A PORTRAIT OF NAPA AND SONOMA ❧ A N D Y   K A T Z ❧ INTRODUCTION BY ROBERT MONDAVI

Published in 1995 by Frequent Flyer Press, Boulder

303-444-5925

Printed and bound in Italy by Arnoldo Mondadori Editore

Library of Congress Catalog Number:

95-95260

To my parents Ed and Emily,

my wife Kathy and son Jesse

❦

FOR YOUR LOVE AND SUPPORT

INTRODUCTION

❦

The Napa Valley and Sonoma regions of Northern California are truly twice blessed—they produce some of the finest wines in the world and the beauty of their landscapes and architecture also rank with the most attractive anywhere. ❦ When I built the Robert Mondavi Winery in 1966, there were perhaps three dozen wineries in both counties. I always knew we had the climate, the soils and the grape varieties to produce fine wines more consistently than any other wine region, and the ensuing decades have demonstrated this. In the past 30 years more than 400 wineries have been built to give this area spectacular countryside views and a series of marvelous architectural personalities. ❦ Andy Katz has given us an exciting tour of this land with his distinctive and dramatic photography. Relax and enjoy this bounty.

Robert Mondavi

PREFACE

❦

In 1990 I received an unusual commission. It was to produce a "portrait" of California's Napa and Sonoma wine country. My friend Michael Ditch, the esteemed chef of Michael's American Bistro of Vail, Colorado, commissioned this portrait to bring some of the rolling hills of the wine country to his restaurant in the rugged mountains of Colorado. ❦ It was only a matter of time until I was drawn back, again and again, to the magnificent landscapes, striking architecture, extraordinary cuisine, distinguished people, and of course, *the wine*. Over the past six years I have photographed this area from dawn until dusk. I have experienced many seasons and countless hours with the passionate people who produce some of the finest wines of the world. ❦ That passion—and the celebration of their harvest—is what draws me to one of the most beautiful places on earth. It is my privilege to share this portrait with my friends and many wine lovers the world over.

Andy Katz

PHOTOGRAPHS

12

23

26

42

49

52

54

58

74

90

This book was a labor of love throughout the past six years and there are so many special people I would like to acknowledge. To Michael Ditch—without his love for food and wine, this book would never have happened. Forrest Tancer and Joy Sterling who's warmth and friendship made every trip to Sonoma special. Barry, Audrey, Laurence, and Terry Sterling for your friendship and support. Robert Mondavi for his special contributions. Jean Arnold who's friendship and enthusiasm was never taken for granted. Dawnine Dyer, Doreen Schmid, Laurie "The Puze" Puzo, John Martini, Zach Berkowitz (the best Jewish farmer in the valley), Ed Farver, thanks for the bubbles! Jan Shrem who has always supported my art. John (Ribbet) and Julie Williams, John and Janet Trefethen, Jeff Jaegar, Ralph Colona, Joy Kagele, Jim Allen, Brent "The Coach" Shortridge, Jack and Jamie Davies, Don and Rhonda Carano, Michael and Jackie Martini, Lou and Helena Foppiano, Bob Foley, Jim and Carolyn Pride, Stuart Bryant, Peter and Su Hua Newton, John Kongsgaard, Elaine Prinz, John Maxwell, Carissa Chappellet, Bruce Cohn, Bob Roux, Larry Brooks, Vivian Gay, Bob Broman, Eugenia Keegan, Orville MaGoon, Jack Stoakes, Eileen Crane, Peter Haywood, Michael and Elaine Honig, Steve and Carol Girard, Jan Stuebing, Brian Larky, Manfred Esser, Bill and Sandra MacIver, Dan Goldfield, Chris and Sanda Howell, Robert and Susan Katz, and the many people I forgot to mention. I would also like to thank Sandra Demiene Knecht and Vermilion Design of Boulder, for their enthusiastic participation in shaping and designing this book.

❧

"To all of you my friends, I tip my glass."

PHOTOGRAPHS

13	Clos Pegase Winery	35	Pinot Noir
14	Iron Horse Vineyards	36	Schramsberg Vineyards
15	Iron Horse Vineyards	37	Schramsberg Vineyards
16	Jordan Vineyard and Winery	38	Kendall Jackson Vineyards, Alexander Valley
17	Jordan Vineyard and Winery		
18	Sebastiani Vineyard, Cherry Block	39	Kendall Jackson Vineyards, Alexander Valley
19	Cain Vineyard and Winery		
20	Kendall Jackson Vineyards, Mount Veeder	40	St. Supery Vineyards and Winery, Pope Valley
21	Niebaum-Coppola Estate Winery	43	Jordan Vineyard and Winery
22	Pinot Noir	44	Opus One
23	Pinot Noir and Zinfandel	45	Domaine Carneros
24	Zinfandel	46	Carneros Creek Winery
27	Clos Pegase Winery	47	Pride Mountain Vineyards
28	Carneros	48	Michelle Schlumburger
29	Pinot Noir	49	Ferrari-Carano Winery
30	Carneros	50	Buena Vista, Carneros
31	Carneros	51	Newton Vineyard
32	Jordan Vineyard and Winery	52	Napa Demtos Cooperage
33	Quail's Ridge Cellars and Vineyards	53	Napa Demtos Cooperage
34	Silverado Trail	54	Clos Pegase Winery

PHOTOGRAPHS

55   Ferrari-Carano Winery

56   Robert Mondavi Winery

59   Clos Pegase Winery

60   Pinot Noir

61   Pinot Noir

62   Yountville

63   Silverado Trail

64   Merlot

65   Chardonnay

66   Domaine Chandon

67   Iron Horse Vineyards

68   Louis Martini Winery, Monte Rossa

69   B.R. Cohn Winery, Olive Hill

70   Pinot Noir

71   Pinot Noir and Chardonnay

72   Hess Collection Winery,
Mount Veeder

74   St. Supery Vineyards and Winery,
Pope Valley

75   Cain Vineyards

76   Domaine Chandon

77   Jordan Vineyard and Winery

78   Jordan Vineyard and Winery

79   T Bar T Ranch

80   Cain Vineyards

81   Carneros

82   Sterling Vineyards

83   Louis Martini Winery, Monte Rossa

84   Rutherford

85   Silver Oak Wine Cellars

86   Domaine Chandon

87   Trefethan Vineyards

88   Yountville

89   Calistoga

91   Newton

Cameras used:
Mamiya RZ67, Mamiya Six
Contax RX, Contax G1

Printed on Durst AC800 and L1200